Connect

to the
whispers
of your soul

Dr. Debra Ford Msc. D

Author: Dr. Debra Ford Msc.D, inspirational teacher and spiritual mystic
Editor: John C. Ford M, charismatic adventurer and intellectual lateral thinker
Author photo: Vanessa Sikomas, spiritual balance and spiritual mystic

Publisher: Energy Mountain Inc.
716 brookpark drive sw, calgary, ab, Canada, t2w 2x4
T: 403.998.0191 and 1.877.866.2086
E: info@SolePath.org
W: www.SolePath.org

Library and Archives Canada Cataloguing in Publication

Ford, Debra, 1957-, author
Connect to the whispers of your soul / Dr. Debra Ford.

Issued in print and electronic formats.
ISBN 978-0-9937517-0-7

DEDICATION

to the four, the core.

CONTENTS

ACKNOWLEDGMENTS

You are my inspiration, thank you for finding your way to this incredible body of work called SolePath.

For John, my love and gratitude.

For Joel and Adam, my sons.

For Deneen, Seth's butterfly.

For Terry, our thanks and friendship.

SECTION 1 - THE DIVINE WAY

You have a deep yearning to connect with your higher self,
to hear and understand the whispers of your soul,
to clearly receive your messages from god,
your guides, your angels,
your soul.

SECTION 1 - THE DIVINE WAY

Revelation #1: Connecting to divine energy is about who you are and who you will be, not only what you will do.

You have a deep yearning to connect with your higher self, to hear and understand the whispers of your soul, to clearly receive your messages from god, your guides, your angels, your soul. You are born with a deep connection to divine energy, yet as you grow older and live your life, this connection becomes unclear, it becomes a fainter quieter voice, as you doubt your ability to identify the subtle whispers.

In early childhood you have a real sense of who you are, of your greatness, of your possibility, and this shows up in your play and in your imagination. As you grow up you are impacted by outside factors including your family, your nationality and your religion. Other people in your life come to have a greater influence over you than your inner voice. Authority figures, societal norms and friends tell you what to do, what to think, and how to feel. From having a real sense of your unique greatness you move to a desire to belong, to fit in and as a result to a place of forgetting who you really are.

As an adult these external factors continue their influence in your life through other experts, your life partner, your boss, the books that seem to be written by those smarter than you, even internet searching. You learn from others what is right and wrong for you, and what is right and wrong about you and all of this serves to cause you to forget who you are, to overlook your own gifts and greatness, and to disregard the unique and personal whispers of your soul.

The credence you give these outside factors is the cause of your disconnection from source energy, from your divine self.

Yet all of you receive messages, all of you can connect to the whispers of your soul for guidance, all of you can reconnect with your higher self.

Receiving messages can be about being directed, about getting answers, about hearing what to do. It can be about knowing how to make your next move, how to act, whether to turn left or whether to turn right.

But surprisingly, the fundamental beauty of being able to receive and interpret the wisdom from your soul is also about knowing who you are, having the life experience your soul intended, understanding the purpose of your life and appreciating your impact on others.

Connecting to non-physical energy is about being, not only about doing.

Revelation #2: It is only possible to connect to the wisdom of divine energy from a place of expanded energy.

In tortured times, that's when you remember to ask spirit for help, when things are going wrong. You ask for guidance when you are confused because you have reached a major crossroads in your life. You ask for guidance when life is sad and perhaps a little out of control. You often ask for guidance as a last resort.

Of course, these are valid reasons to connect for divine wisdom and spirit would certainly like to help at these times, but it is almost impossible to receive clarity when you feel this way. It is impossible to connect to the whispers of your soul when you are experiencing negative emotions like fear and despair. It is impossible to get clear guidance when you are in this place of collapsed energy.

Finding a way to move from this place of collapsed energy to expanded energy even when life feels difficult and confusing, is the only way for you to connect. It is only from a place of expanded energy that you can receive divine guidance; this is the only place where there is clarity for you.

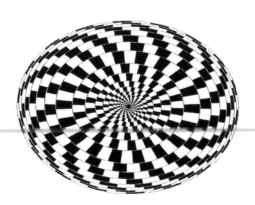

Revelation #3: You connect to non-physical energy in a subtle way that is personal, unique and divinely yours.

You may also have preconceived notions about when and how your messages will arrive. Some of you say 'why can't it be a billboard in the sky'; 'why can't it be loud and clear'? Yet there is a beauty and a subtlety around the way that the divine interacts with you. There are ways that are specific to you and your SolePath that provide the path for you to connect to the whispers of your soul.

Your subtle guidance may be the urge to stop on the highway to watch a beautiful sky, and then to continue on your journey five minutes later. What was that delay for; what were you being guided away from; what were you being guided towards? The road you are travelling on is completely different five minutes later.

"Let Me explain something to you. You have this idea that God shows up in only one way in life. That's a very dangerous idea. It stops you from seeing God all over. If you think God looks only one way or sounds only one way or is only one way, you're going to look right past Me night and day. You'll spend your whole life looking for God and not finding Her. Because you're looking for a Him."

Conversations with God: An Uncommon Dialogue, Book 1, by
Neale Donald Walsch

Revelation #4: You have to ask for divine help.

Let's consider the three fundamental questions of life to help with the understanding that communicating with divine energy can be a simple fact of life. It is an ability, that you all have, that can be part of your everyday existence. But you have to ask for help.

Question number one; 'who am I?'

You are a perfect eternal soul, having a deliberate, carefully planned physical incarnation. Before you are born you create a plan for your lifetime, a plan that provides you with the perfect soul experience, a plan that includes your SolePath, your expanded energy and your collapsed energy.

Your plan is not created in isolation; it is written with the agreement and assistance of your soul family. There is nothing in your plan, in your life experience that you cannot cope with and your soul community is standing by all the time, to help whenever you need them.

Your plan is made up of fixed parts, those things that you cannot change, such as your gender, your genealogy, your age, your nationality, and this is called your destiny. Your plan also includes parts that are changeable, the choices that you make, such as who to marry, what job to take, where to live and this is called your free will and is the life that you are actively creating.

Divine help is there for all parts of your life; for assistance with your free will choices and for assistance with accepting your destiny. Most importantly, not only can you ask for assistance, but you must ask for help because divine will only engage when you ask.

`Revelation # 5: Make it a habit; connect in the good times and the bad times.

Question number two: 'what am I doing here?'

You come to earth to experience contrast or what you do not want. It is only in the experiencing of what you do <u>not</u> want, that you can know what you <u>do</u> want. You come to earth to experience collapsed energy, your DarkPath, your place of personal growth. You come to earth to experience choosing something better, choosing expanded energy, your LightPaths. It is only from this place of expanded energy that you are connected to your soul, to your higher self, to your fundamental wisdom, to your life's purpose.

You are living lives that give you the perfect opportunity to consciously and deliberately choose away from your collapsed energy, your DarkPath. Lives that provide the chance to choose your LightPaths; lives that give you moment-by-moment options to choose away from your collapsed energy, from what you do not want. Lives that allow you to interact with others in expanded energy, to become who you were born to be.

ALL IS WELL AND IF YOU AREN'T FEELING POSITIVE, JOYFUL, HAPPY, IT IS INCUMBENT ON YOU TO REACH FOR A BETTER FEELING. THIS IS YOUR ONLY ACTION; THIS MUST BE YOUR ONLY GOAL. ALL OF YOUR LIFE IS YOUR CREATION OR YOUR DESTINY; YOU ARE ONLY ON EARTH TO CHOOSE JOY AS YOU NAVIGATE THROUGH THESE EXPERIENCES. WE UNDERSTAND THE DIFFICULTY IN THIS, TRULY WE DO, AND YOU ARE ALL DOING SO WELL UNDER THE CIRCUMSTANCES. WE ARE WITH YOU, WITH ALL OF YOU, ALL OF THE TIME. CHOOSE JOY; MAKE A CONSCIOUS DELIBERATE CHOICE FOR JOY.

SETH

And joy is what you say it is.

Your uncomfortable or difficult life experiences are important moments, not just as growth opportunities, but it is usually in these moments of dark energetic collapse that you remember to call upon divine energy for help.

Yet, you can learn to ask for guidance, to hear the whispers of your soul, not only when you despair but also when life is flowing.

↖ ↗

Everything I am not
Made me everything I am

↙ ↘

Revelation #6: When you connect, it impacts you and all of us.

Question number three: 'who will I be in relation to what is going on around me?'

In every moment of every day, in every situation you are faced with choices. All of these choices have an outcome, or behaviour. This is one of the fundamental questions 'who will I be in relation to what is going on around me?' Every thought, feeling, action is a choice.

A situation arises that triggers a thought and emotion. You become aware of your thought and emotion and choose to hold onto that or not. In the moment of your awareness, you participate in choosing. When you deliberately choose withholding thought and emotion, you are deliberately steering yourself toward negative behaviour. This negative behaviour will always have a poor effect on someone else, maybe not in the moment, but at some time.

One choice of positive behaviour, of loving actions, has an enormous impact on the all. This is the secret to your incarnation, to each of you choosing to be on earth. Seth

Yet might it not be just a little easier to choose positive behaviour that positively impacts yourself and others if you could hear the whispers of your soul? If you could call upon the help you need in all your interactions with others?

Revelation #7: Your SolePath categories provide the way to hear the whispers of your soul.

There are 22 SolePaths, divided into 6 categories. For each of you, your SolePath is a braid of two LightPaths and one DarkPath. Your LightPaths and DarkPath each belong to a category, or a group classification. In your own, unique, personal SolePath braid you may have three categories, two categories or one category and these are the overall guide to how you interact with the physical and non-physical world.

Category	SolePath
Charismatic category	adventurer, gladiator, influencer, leader, performer
Compassionate category	caretaker, facilitator, healer
Inspirational category	conformist, humanitarian, manager, teacher
Intellectual category	controller, expert, lateral thinker
Intuitive category	builder, creator, hunter, solitude
Spiritual category	balance, mystic, warrior

Revelation #8: Both your LightPath and DarkPath categories provide connection to divine energy.

The analysis of a SolePath is a mystical process and is completed using dowsing rods. The first reading, completed by a SolePath certified energy analyst, is to measure the energy of the categories and this is followed by a second reading to identify, within those categories, the two LightPaths and one DarkPath.

All of the categories that apply to an individual's SolePath exhibit expanded energy and this is regardless of whether the categories contain the two LightPaths or the one DarkPath. What we understand from this energetic reading is that even for the DarkPath, the category represents expanded energy.

Both your LightPaths and DarkPath are made up of a category and a SolePath. For example you may be a compassionate caretaker, or a compassionate healer. Compassionate is the category that includes group or shared characteristics, healer and caretaker include specific characteristics for that particular SolePath.

In the metaphysical sense, your DarkPath is a past life completion, it is a familiar skill that has a 'been there, done that' energy around it. For your DarkPath, the category is of benefit to you (as a familiar skill) when it is used to support your LightPaths.

If you are a dark charismatic you may be even more sparkly than a light charismatic as you are more familiar with your charisma; you may be better at lighting up a room; you may be a more engaging person. This is possible because of the many lifetimes of past experience.

If you are a dark compassionate you may have an even greater capacity to love than a light compassionate. If you are a dark inspirational you may have a greater ability to get things done, to be relied upon than a light inspirational. If you are a dark intellectual you may have a greater capacity for logical, rational thought than a light intellectual. If you are a dark intuitive you may be better able to recognize your gut feelings than a light intuitive. If you are a dark spiritual you may connect more easily than a light spiritual.

Your DarkPath is your place of personal growth, your LightPaths are your path to purpose and living the life your soul intended. Your DarkPath provides you with choices whether to engage in life from a place of collapsed energy or whether to reach for expanded energy.

Connecting to your soul is only possible when you are in expanded energy. Of course, this is when you are responding to the world from your LightPaths and now you understand that you can also use your DarkPath category to connect too. Your DarkPath category is the light of your DarkPath.

SOLEPATH IS A TEACHING THAT IS DIRECTIONAL — GIVING A FRAMEWORK TO AN EARTH INCARNATION. SOLEPATH PROVIDES A MEANS FOR NAVIGATION OVER THE COURSE OF A LIFETIME. SETH

CONTEMPLATION

1. Why does your soul wish to communicate with you?

2. Are you receiving messages now? What are those messages?

3. How do you recognize your messages?

4. Are they physical sensations like tickles, coughs, sneezes, pains?

5. Do they come through your five senses?

6. Do you recognize your messages in a different way?

7. When do you primarily receive your messages? Is it a particular time of day? Are there specific circumstances?

8. Do you receive messages while you sleep? What are they like? How are they different?

9. Were you more aware of divine energy as a child? How did this show up for you?

10. Was there a life event that you remember that connected you to your LightPaths; that was divinely guided?

11. Was there a life event that disconnected you from the divine?

12. Have you experienced any miracles in your life? A narrow escape or an event that defies explanation.

13. What has been the subtle guidance in your life?

14. What has been the overt guidance in your life?

SYNOPSIS

Revelation #1: Connecting to divine energy is about who you are and who you will be, not only what you will do.

Revelation #2: It is only possible to connect to the wisdom of divine energy from a place of expanded energy.

Revelation #3: You connect to non-physical energy in a subtle way that is personal, unique and divinely yours.

Revelation #4: You have to ask for divine help.

Revelation # 5: Make it a habit; connect in the good times and the bad times. *Soul evolution. Dark there for growth. Choice*

Revelation #6: When you connect, it impacts you and all of us.

Revelation #7: Your SolePath categories provide the way to hear the whispers of your soul.

Revelation #8: Both your LightPath and DarkPath categories provide connection to divine energy.

Dark such a mastered skill

SECTION 2 - YOUR WAY

You have unique and personal ways to reliably receive messages
from the divine; and you can be aware of and understand
this connection to your soul, your higher self,
your guides, your god.

SECTION 2 - YOUR WAY

Your 'I Am ...'

In ancient cultures, including Hebrew, Christian and indigenous spirituality, the word for god is the same as "I Am". When you state "I Am", using your SolePath categories you are connecting to yourself at a profound, fundamental and deep level.

Energetically, your SolePath "I Am" is a way to align yourself with divine energy, to create a matching vibration with the all that is. For each category, "I Am" statements are based on the Tao.

The Tao depicts the building blocks of the creative energy of the universe; it is your being-ness; your deep knowing that you are more than your physical body and that the purpose of your life on earth is the evolution of your soul.

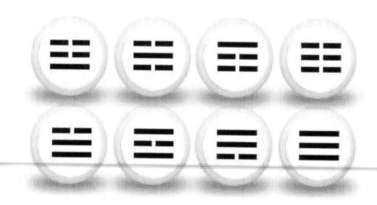

Here are the "I Am" statements for each SolePath category. They will be combined with a breath exercise later on, as a tool to help you connect to divine wisdom.

For the charismatic category:

I Am charismatic and I Am bright and aware

The trigram of the Tao for the charismatic category SolePaths is fire. Fire denotes change; it is hot, explosive, bright, clear and enlightened.

For the compassionate category:

I Am compassionate and I Am confident and deep

The trigram of the Tao for the compassionate category SolePaths is water. Water denotes depth; is flowing, fluid, reflective and sometimes still.

For the inspirational category:

I Am inspirational and I Am powerful and free

The trigram of the Tao for the inspirational category SolePaths is thunder. Thunder denotes release; it is abrupt, loud, powerful and heralds nourishment.

For the intellectual category:

I Am intellectual and I Am curious and connected

The trigram of the Tao for the intellectual category SolePaths is wind. Wind is always moving, gentle, yet can be strong and unsettling.

For the intuitive category:

I Am intuitive and I Am fun and full

The trigram of the Tao for the intuitive category SolePaths is lake. Lake is contained joy and has depth without overflowing.

For the spiritual category:

I Am spiritual and I am strong, steady and wise.

The trigram of the Tao for the spiritual category SolePaths is the mountain. The mountain denotes constancy; it is everlasting, durable, all seeing and always there.

Understanding how you receive your messages

Each SolePath category has a unique and particular way of connecting to soul and to divine energy.

You have unique and personal ways to reliably receive the messages from the divine; and you can be aware of and understand these key ways to connect to your soul, your higher self, your guides, your god.

You have key communication words and phrases that can help with the interpretation of the subtle whispers of your soul.

You have a place on your physical body that provides a direct connection to your soul. A physical body part that when you place your attention and awareness on it, links you to your fundamental wisdom.

Charismatic category SolePaths: *3%*
adventurer, gladiator, influencer, leader, performer

Charismatics are the world's 'sparkle' people who navigate to success, joy and purpose with outgoing sensing and perception. Just like a bat they are able to interpret the returning echoes from life. Their contribution to the world is their light.

Receiving messages:

As a charismatic SolePath, you are most effective when you take the time to review, reflect and observe. You are a visual learner so pay attention to the images in your world, those that are relevant to you and your life experience. *Best judge of Character*

The key communication words for charismatics are 'sense' and 'reflect'.

When assessing signs, symbols, images and other messages from divine energy ask,

- What is being reflected here?
- Am I reflecting someone else's truth, or is this my instinct? Is this 'mine' or 'theirs'?
- What am I sensing?

Place on the physical body that connects directly to the charismatic soul: your skin, which is the largest organ in your body, and regulates and protects your physical body.

Compassionate category SolePaths:
caretaker, facilitator, healer

> Compassionates are the 'love' people who navigate to success, joy and purpose through their heart. Filling the world with their extraordinary ability to show love and compassion. Their contribution to the world is their capacity to love.

Receiving messages:

As a compassionate SolePath, your learning style is participatory, experiential and kinesthetic. You are a hands-on learner so get involved and pay attention to your life's experiences, those that feel relevant to you and those that don't.

The key communication words for compassionates are 'feel' and 'love'.

When assessing signs, symbols, images and other messages from divine energy ask,

- What do I feel?
- Does this feel loving?
- Is this how I feel or someone else's opinion?

Place on the physical body that connects directly to the compassionate soul: your heart, which pumps life into all parts of your body.

Inspirational SolePaths:
conformist, humanitarian, manager, teacher

Inspirationals are the world's role models who ask 'what does the world need and how can I provide it?' Their success, joy and purpose lies in their desire to make a difference, to serve, to help. Their contribution to the world is their desire to be the change.

Receiving messages:

As an inspirational SolePath, you are a visual learner who likes to see that you have accomplished something worthwhile. Your most effective learning comes in practical situations, rather than simply theoretical and abstract.

The key communication words for inspirationals are 'see' and 'look'.

When assessing signs, symbols, images and other messages from divine energy ask,

- What do I see?
- What would I do if I could see the whole picture?
- What would change if I looked up? If I looked ahead?
- Is this how I see or someone else's opinion?

Place on the physical body that connects directly to the inspirational soul: your adrenals, which sit on top of your kidneys and are responsible for balance in your body.

Intellectual SolePaths:
controller, expert, lateral thinker

> Intellectuals are the world's great minds. They navigate to success, joy and purpose through their brain, through their ability to think things through. They push the boundaries of logic and reason and their contribution to the world is their unrestrained moving towards 'more' and 'better'.

Receiving messages:

As an intellectual SolePath, your learning style is auditory and theoretical. You are a logical learner who likes to discuss both sides of the equation. To hear the messages of your soul, practice listening, not talking.

The key communication word for intellectuals is 'think'.

When assessing signs, symbols, images and other messages from divine energy ask,

- What do I think?
- What is the logical next step? What is the logical outcome?
- Have I taken enough time to think this through?
- Is this what I think or someone else's opinion?

Place on the physical body that connects directly to the intellectual soul: your pineal gland which is in the centre of your brain and is connected to the circadian rhythms of night and day, responsible for your natural patterns and routine.

Intuitive SolePaths:
builder, creator, hunter, solitude

Intuitives are the 'gut' feeling people who navigate to success, joy and purpose through their immediate body wisdom. They are ideas people and their body and its responses are their guide, they just know when things are right. Their contribution to the world is wisdom, knowing and their incredible ideas.

Receiving messages:

As an intuitive SolePath, your learning style is experiential, hands-on and kinesthetic. You are a hands-on learner so get involved in life and pay attention to your life's experiences, those that you know are relevant to you and those that aren't.

The key communication word for intuitives is 'know'.

When assessing signs, symbols, images and other messages from divine energy ask,

- What do I know?
- If I knew the answer to this, what would it be?
- What was my first reaction, I know that I can trust that?
- Is this my knowing or someone else's opinion?

Place on the physical body that connects directly to the intuitive soul: your gut, your core, your solar plexus, which is the location of your connection to the field of energy.

27

Spiritual SolePaths:
balance, mystic, warrior

A metaphysical explorer who navigates to success, joy and purpose through their fearless look at 'what you cannot see'. They push the boundaries of beliefs and their contribution to our world is their deep desire to explore the invisible.

Receiving messages:

As a spiritual SolePath, your learning style is conceptual, abstract and uses metaphysical impressions. You are a good listener and an auditory learner. Speak about your connection experiences, sometimes you need to be the one talking, not always the one listening.

The key communication words for spirituals are 'connect' and 'get'.

When assessing signs, symbols, images and other messages from divine energy ask,

- What am I getting (from non-physical help) with regard to this situation?
- Is this my download from my connection, or the opinion of someone else?

Place on the physical body that connects directly to the spiritual soul: your third eye, which is your ability to perceive beliefs and what is invisible.

CONTEMPLATION

1. How do your SolePath categories help you receive your messages?

2. What action can you take, right here, right now to experience your particular learning style?

3. What can you do to better notice your audio, visual or kinesthetic connection?

4. How can you use your key communication words to better understand the divine guidance you receive?

5. What can you do to gain a deeper understanding of the physical place on your body that connects directly to your soul? How can you put your attention and focus here?

6. What is the difference when you connect to the divine using your LightPath categories or your DarkPath category?

7. What experiences in your life have you had?

SECTION 3 - OUR WAY

Choosing
Matching
Connecting
Asking

Your unique and personal ways to
reliably receive messages
from the divine.

SECTION 3 – OUR WAY

Choosing

Your connection to divine guidance is only possible when you live in expanded energy. The way that you know whether you are responding from a place of expansion or a place of collapse is through emotion. All it takes is a simple awareness of your emotion; of what you are feeling in the moment. Right here, right now, are your emotions positive or negative?

Sometimes you just feel sad, you simply get angry, you surrender to stress, you succumb to outside factors, people, experiences, events, that make you feel bad. When you are feeling negative emotions, understand that there is an unconscious choosing to feel this way. Your emotions do not come from outside of you, they are within you and are within your control.

Situations arise that trigger your habitual negative emotions, which then come to the surface without your conscious awareness. Become aware of your negative emotions, become aware that this is an unconscious choice, become aware that these negative emotions are causing your disconnection from your divine self, from your clarity and answers.

Expanded and collapsed energy emotions are easy to identify using the emotion zones below.

Emotion zones:

Expanded energy	Expanded energy
Active positive emotions	Passive positive emotions
Feeling happy, loving, joyful, cheerful, playful, bright, delighted, thankful, dynamic, eager, inspired, excited, enthusiastic, bold	Feeling content, safe, peaceful, satisfied, comfortable, relaxed, serene, free, certain, optimistic, confident, hopeful, calm, blessed
Collapsed energy	Collapsed energy
Active negative emotions	Passive negative emotions
Feeling angry, in despair, sulky, frustrated, wronged, frightened, worried, fearful, suspicious, panicked, threatened, offended, afflicted, bullying	Feeling victimized, depressed, powerless, ashamed, disappointed, discouraged, dissatisfied, lost, nervous, timid, doubtful, wary, rejected, injured

Choosing to make a divine connection is about understanding the impact of your negative emotions and how they disconnect you from your wisdom. First become aware of your emotion. Second, understand that you are unconsciously choosing your negative emotion. Third, choose not to feel this way.

And all of this choosing away from negative emotion can only take place from the moment. Connection cannot take place from the past or from the future, only from the now. It is important to remember that it is only from this moment that it is possible to connect to divine energy. Right here, right now, it begins with choosing positive emotion.

IF I TAKE THE NEXT STEP TO FEELING BETTER, THAT I ALLOW SPIRIT, ENERGY, DESTINY, GOD, MY ANGELS, MY GUIDES, MY HIGHER SELF, MY SOUL, TO BRING TO ME ALL THAT IS IN MY PLAN.

HOW YOU REACH THE BEST OUTCOME AND POTENTIAL IN YOUR LIFE IS TO CHOOSE A BETTER FEELING IN THE MOMENT AND TO TAKE THE NEXT BEST STEP. SETH

Step one: choosing *emotions not to us by us.*

State — "I don't want to feel this way".

Saying 'I don't want to feel this way' is stating that you do not want to unconsciously choose this negative emotion; emotion that disconnects you from your soul, your god, your guides, your angels.

Matching

You have chosen not to unconsciously experience your negative emotion and your next step is to move from collapsed energy to expanded energy. Expanded energy is created by positive emotion.

Sometimes emotion can be confusing. For example, love often comes with attachments; 'I am loved when I behave this way'; 'I am loved when I look this way'. It could be difficult to discern what is a positive emotion and what is a negative emotion. But finding a positive emotion to match is an easy way to quickly move to expanded energy.

The clearest positive emotions to match are thankfulness (active positive) or serenity (passive positive). Most people can easily replicate the expanding emotions of thankfulness, gratitude or appreciation; or serenity, flow or acceptance.

"As the infinite creator of your life you may also look at the contrast you are experiencing and then choose a better experience." JANE

Step two: matching

Create expanding energy, match the positive emotions of thankfulness or serenity.

Connecting

Each SolePath category has a meditative breath exercise that connects you to your divine wisdom. Each category meditation exercise brings you to the moment, to the now, as it is only from this moment that you can connect for guidance. You cannot connect from the past or from the future. First priority of your category breath exercise is to bring you to the now.

Your SolePath category breath exercise places your focus on the body part that connects you directly to the divine. This is a physical place on your body that as you place your attention and focus there, connects you to your soul. Second priority of the breath exercise is to focus on your body's soul connection.

Third priority of your SolePath category breath exercise is your unique and personal "I Am" statement, aligning you with divine energy and the matching vibration of all that is.

This breath exercise can be done anywhere, any place and takes no more than 60 seconds. Get familiar with it by first creating a meditative attitude. Sit quietly and close your eyes softly with your eyelids relaxed. Relax your jaw, soften your lips and feel your scalp calming.

Notice the breath going in and out of your body, cooler as it goes in, warmer as it comes out. Imagine that you are breathing in bright white light that is filling up your body. Imagine that you are breathing out dark energy that you no longer need.

Making your charismatic connection to divine energy:

> Breathe in and breathe out, imagine that you are inside a shell, like the shell of an egg, and place your focus on this safe, exterior covering. Breathe in and breathe out, and state
> "I Am charismatic and I Am bright and aware."

Making your compassionate connection to divine energy:

> Breathe in and breathe out, place your hand and your focus on your heart. Breathe in and breathe out, and state
> "I Am compassionate and I Am confident and deep."

Making your inspirational connection to divine energy:

> Breathe in and breathe out, place your hands and your focus on your adrenal glands (which sit on top of your kidneys in the middle of your back on either side of your spine). Straighten your spine, then breathe in and breathe out, and state
> "I Am inspirational and I Am powerful and free."

Making your intellectual connection to divine energy:

Breathe in and breathe out, place your focus and attention on your pineal gland (shaped like a tiny pine cone, between the two hemispheres near the centre of your brain). Breathe in and breathe out, and state
"I Am intellectual and I Am curious and connected."

Lake

Making your intuitive connection to divine energy:

Breathe in and breathe out, place your hand and your focus on your solar plexus. Breathe in and breathe out, and state
"I Am intuitive and I Am fun and full."

Making your spiritual connection to divine energy:

Breathe in and breathe out, place your attention and your focus on your third eye (the space between your eyebrows). Breathe in and breathe out, and state
"I Am spiritual and I Am strong, steady and wise."

At different times, try using each of your SolePath categories. Become aware of the differences in the connection between your LightPath and DarkPath categories; whether your connection process is easier from one category or another; whether you receive a different kind of wisdom and guidance depending on the category.

No matter what SolePath categories you have, when you are living in expanded energy, experiencing positive emotion, you are connected to the whispers of your soul. Each of you simply has different ways to navigate to your connection to divine energy.

As Seth says, you are safe and all is well.

Step three: connecting

Breathe in and breathe out, place your attention and your focus on your body connection. Breathe in and breathe out, and state your "I Am" statement

Asking

You have decided not to unconsciously choose collapsed energy or negative emotion, stating, "I don't want to feel this way". You have found a way to create expanded energy for yourself by matching your vibration to the familiar positive emotions of thankfulness or serenity. You have created a meditative attitude of quietness with your breath bringing yourself to the now, focusing on the body part of your SolePath categories and connecting to your higher self using your "I Am".

Next step is to ask for help as god, your angels, your guides will only engage when asked to help. Traditional prayers or mantras, inspiring texts or personal favourite prayers can be used.

Here are some suggestions for asking for help:

1. If you are facing a challenge, ask for help and for trust
2. If you are living with hardship, ask for ease and possibility
3. If you are worried, ask for peace and clarity
4. If you are afraid, ask to feel safe and for growth
5. If you are sick, ask for health and balance
6. If you are lonely, ask for companionship and to feel worthy
7. If you are lost, ask for direction and for decisions
8. If you are unsupported, ask for strength and for faith
9. If you are living with disharmony, ask for kindness and healthy connections

Or try using these prayers:

> Balance and revive me, heal my body, my heart and my
> mind

> Grant me no judgment, no expectations, complete trust

> Guide me to manifest my gifts and my greatness

> Give me courage to face the day, to remember that I am a
> perfect eternal soul

Serenity prayer:

> God grant me the serenity to accept the things I cannot change;
> courage to change the things I can; and the wisdom to know the
> difference.

Step four: asking

Ask for divine assistance.

SYNOPSIS

Step one: choosing

>
> State — "I don't want to feel this way"

Step two: matching

>
> Create expanding energy,
>
> match the positive emotions of thankfulness or serenity.

Step three: connecting

>
> Breathe in and breathe out,
>
> place your attention and
>
> your focus on your body connection.
>
> Breathe in and breathe out,
>
> and state your "I Am" statement.

Step four: asking

>
> Ask for help, for ease, for peace, to feel safe,
>
> for health, for companionship, for direction,
>
> for strength, for kindness, for what you need.

SECTION 4 - INSPIRATION

The purpose of your life is living in a better feeling thought moment by moment. It is only from this moment that you create the future outcome.

Seth

SECTION 4 - INSPIRATION

Seth transcript: 180 of intentions

John: This is a Seth session on Wednesday, November 20, 2013 with Liz, John & Seth.

SETH: GOOD MORNING,

Liz: Good morning!

SETH: YOU ARE WELCOME HERE WITH ME.

Liz: Oh wonderful, thank you

SETH: YOU HAVE QUESTIONS AROUND CREATION OF YOUR LIFE, YES?

Liz: Yes

SETH: YOU MAY ASK.

Liz: Well, the main question I had is if you could offer me any guidance on planting seeds for the future wisely. I feel like I have recently been reaching for the light and at times reaching for better feeling thoughts and seeing where that leads without a crystal clear intention, a material intention for how things might look. And I am just wondering if you can offer any guidance about planting seeds wisely because it can almost feel a little reckless doing that, given in the past, I've had a full vision of where I'm going, but I don't have a vision any more now of where I am going and I don't know what my future will look like and I guess I always thought I would.

Seth: Well you have found yourself and vibrated yourself to the perfect energy of creation and so it is important for you to have future vision and future goals, but what many of you have forgotten is that it is only in the moment that you are creating. And so reaching for that better feeling thought in this moment creates the next moment of a better feeling thought. And so, you are all striving for purpose and striving for that thing that you will do, in effect, **the purpose of your life is living in a better feeling thought moment by moment. It is only from this moment that you create the future outcome** and you have already experienced, dear soul, the ability of spirit to bring more to you than you could have imagined. You have already felt this in your life, yes?

Liz: Yes, yes, yes, yes.

2:59 Seth: and so that it is good to have a future intention in a way that it is soothing, but it is not the way that you reach the purpose and the meaning and the outcome of why you are choosing to live an incarnation on this planet. So that the work is done from the moment and it is so that in the 2012 energy shift, the vibration on your planet changed significantly that you will only know as spiritual energies the outcome of what this was from 20 years future, looking back, but this past energy that you have come through, which was the yang energy, was about doing and stating and striving for future intentions, but **the energy you live in now is about a moment by moment choice of something better and this is how you guide to purpose.** The piece that you will struggle with is the letting go of how it used to be. And so that you feel reckless, is it possible for you to define that emotion as free, freedom.

4:40 Liz: That makes me want to ask that if even, let's say, you're at work and you're having a stressful moment or dealing with a challenge that you really don't know how to deal with, its just challenging and you kind of engage all your tools, given what you're just saying, would it be relevant and apparent to just stop, and take a breath, look for what feels better right now?   Maybe you look around or hear a bird out the window or, anything to just take your mind off and to raise your vibration, and if so, can that be trusted?

Seth: Well, will you? Will you trust this? But it is only about reaching for a better feeling and sometimes a better feeling is peace, contentment, gratitude and sometimes a better feeling is simple surrender, simple awareness that what I am feeling is not who I am and where I want to be and so that this is the journey of life, you are all moving towards service of others, towards engaging with others in a light way, energetically expanded way, and this is the path to purpose and so it seems so simple, yes, and so difficult when one is at work and engaged in a difficult situation.

6:46 Liz: And what about in personal life being fearful that things won't work out the way you want them to be in the future?

7: 10 Seth: And so things won't work out the way you want them to be in the future is the old paradigm and the new paradigm is that if I take the next step to feeling better, that I allow spirit, energy, destiny, God, my angels, my guides, my higher self, my soul, to bring to me all that is in my plan. It is through the fear, the blocking, it is not through the managing of what it

MUST LOOK LIKE AND SO WE JOKE OFTEN THAT IF YOU DID NOT WRITE WINNING THE LOTTERY INTO YOUR PLAN, YOU MAY BUY AS MANY LOTTERY TICKETS AS YOU WISH, BUT THIS IS AN OLD PARADIGM, YES? SO THAT YOU WILL LEAVE AN OPENING FOR SPIRIT TO BRING YOU MORE THAN YOU COULD IMAGINE, THE WAY THAT YOU DO THIS IS RIGHT HERE, RIGHT NOW, REACHING FOR MORE EXPANDED ENERGY. THE WAY THAT YOU RECOGNIZE MORE EXPANDED ENERGY IS THROUGH POSITIVE EMOTION. IT IS YOUR ONLY WORK, YES?

Liz: Yes, I guess to feel joy now, in the moment, yes, is that what you are saying?

SETH: YES AND THE TOOL IS TO FIND AN EMOTION THAT IS RECOGNIZABLE FOR YOU, TO FIND SOMETHING THAT IS EASY TO REACH FOR. OTHERS HAVE DESCRIBED IT AS TRANQUILITY, OTHERS HAVE DESCRIBED IT AS FEELING SAFE, SOME HAVE DESCRIBED IT AS A FEELING OF THANKFULNESS SO THAT AN EMOTION THAT IS PURE AND UNCLUTTERED, AS LOVE, AS AN EMOTION COMES WITH MANY ATTACHMENTS, IT IS A DIFFICULT EMOTION TO REACH FOR, BUT IN FINDING THAT THING THAT IS EASY FOR YOU TO FEEL AND TO KNOW, IT IS FAMILIAR AND THEN TO MATCH THAT EMOTION, TO REACH FOR YOUR LIGHT PATHS AND YOUR EXPANDED ENERGY AND SO AS YOU DO THIS IN THE MOMENT BY MOMENT, YOU WOULD ALSO KNOW, WHAT IS MY NEXT BEST STEP. BECAUSE THIS IS IN REALITY, YOUR ONLY TRUTH, YOU CAN ONLY TAKE THE NEXT BEST STEP, THERE ARE TOO MANY INTERSECTIONS IN THE WEB OF THE COLLECTIVE FOR YOU TO MUSCLE WHAT WILL BE YOUR FUTURE OUTCOME SO THAT REACHING FOR AN EMOTION, CHOOSING YOUR NEXT BEST STEP, THAT ALL WILL LEAD TO THIS THING THAT SHE CALLS THE PATH TO PURPOSE AND A BEAUTIFUL LIFE. EASY, YES?

10:20 Liz: Yeah, so reach for a better emotion and choose your next best step.

SETH: HMMM,

Liz: But, you know I heard you earlier mention something about the plan and I believe I heard you say that if it is not in your plan to win the lottery, you can buy as many lottery tickets as you want and you are not going to win it?

SETH: YES, I SAID.

Liz: Really? But are we not infinite creators?

11:00 SETH: I WILL DESCRIBE IT IN TWO WAYS FOR YOU: SO THAT YOU ARE CREATING BEFORE YOU ARE BORN, YES YOU ARE INFINITE CREATORS IS MY ANSWER, BUT YOU ARE, BEFORE YOU ARE BORN CHOOSING THE EXACT LIFE EXPERIENCE THAT WILL BRING TO YOU ALL THAT YOUR SOUL DESIRED IN TERMS OF ITS EVOLUTION, YOUR PERFECT ETERNAL SOUL'S GROWTH AND EXPANSION. THIS IS WHY YOU ARE ON YOUR PLANET, THIS IS THE SCHOOL OF HARD KNOCKS. SO THAT YOU CREATE THIS PLAN WITH ALL OF THESE POTENTIALS; FROM YOUR PHYSICAL INCARNATION YOU SEE IT AS TWO DIMENSIONAL, BUT IT IS FOUR DIMENSIONAL, THERE ARE SO MANY INTERSECTIONS. THERE ARE THINGS THAT ARE IN YOUR PLAN THAT ARE NOT IN YOUR PLAN, BUT **how you reach the best outcome and potential in your life is to choose a better feeling in the moment and to take the next best step.** SO WE FIND IT EASIEST TO DESCRIBE IT AS A TUNNEL, YOUR LIFE'S TUNNEL, AS YOU FLOW THROUGH YOUR TUNNEL YOU ARE FACED WITH PICTURES, YOU ARE FACED WITH CHOICES, PICTURES ON THE WALL OF YOUR TUNNEL AND AS YOU LOOK AT A PICTURE, A NEW SET OF PICTURES OPENS UP, BUT THOSE ARE YOUR PICTURES, THOSE ARE YOUR PLANS. SO, WITHIN YOUR POTENTIALS, WITHIN

THE POTENTIALS THAT ARE YOUR EXISTENCE, YOU ARE AN INFINITE CREATOR, BUT YOU WILL NOT OVERRIDE YOUR SOUL'S PLAN. AND YOUR SOUL HAS PICKED THE PERFECT JOY, LOVE, HAPPINESS, HEALTH, ABUNDANCE; ALL OF THIS EXISTS IN ALL OF THE PLANS.

13:13 Liz: So, given all of this, if we're making choices for our future, I'm going to give an example, if that's okay, 10 years ago, I had a crystal clear plan and I had an intention that I wanted to live a life in a community in a beautiful lush tropical island and live a certain lifestyle so, I made clear decisions, some of which I pained over, whether or not to make to move to Hawaii. And now I am noticing that maybe there is something else, maybe there is somewhere else, I am having experiences that make me think, oh, maybe there's an environment where I'll feel healthier or.... Basically, I'm thinking is that should I or could I be making decisions for what to do in my future and then, well once again, the fear comes in, well if I do this maybe this won't happen. So, given everything that you've been saying I am picking up that I don't have to make decisions for my future, **I just have to feel good right now and trust that each opportunity will be clearly presented to me and I'll know what to do by how I'm feeling in each moment.** Is that true?

SETH: I COULDN'T HAVE EXPRESSED IT BETTER MYSELF. SO THAT, AS 10 YEARS AGO YOU SEE YOURSELF IN A TROPICAL ISLAND IN AN ENVIRONMENT, YOUR SOUL BRINGS TO YOU GLIMPSES OF WHERE YOU ARE HEADED. THERE IS NO WRONG IN WANTING TO, EACH OF YOU DESIRES DIFFERENT THINGS, THERE IS NO WRONG IN DESIRE, BUT WHAT I STATE IS HOW YOU REACH YOUR SOUL'S DESIRE IS EXACTLY AS YOU SAID.

15:50 Liz: okay, so no need to sit down and make a list of pro's and con's and decisions, all I have to do is feel good right now and discern along the way, maybe just notice along the way, hmm, maybe it would be fun to live in a place where there is winter part of the year and see how that turns out. Maybe it might be that I end up having a house in Colorado and another house here, but I don't even have to make decisions or start making plans.

16:30 SETH: YOU WILL FOLLOW THE NEXT BREADCRUMB, YOU WILL TAKE YOUR NEXT BEST STEP.

Liz: **What's my next best step? It's so simple! And so easy!**

SETH: AND IT IS THE VERY SIMPLICITY OF IT THAT WILL BE SO DIFFICULT FOR SOME, BUT NOT FOR YOU, YOU ARE READY. THERE IS A FREEDOM THAT I AM OFFERING YOU.

Liz: Oh, that makes me feel good to hear that.

SETH: BUT YOU ARE GOOD AT THIS, YOU ARE SAFE. YOU ARE GOOD AT... YOUR AWARENESS AROUND HOW YOU ARE FEELING IN THE MOMENT IS VERY HIGH, AND SO THERE ARE STEPS THAT GET YOU TO THE PLACE WHERE YOU SAY 'I WILL CHOOSE A BETTER FEELING' AND IT STARTS WITH AWARENESS. OF COURSE, THERE IS THE SOLEPATH NAVIGATION THAT YOU HAVE CLARITY AROUND WHAT THESE DARK AND LIGHT PARTS OF YOU ARE CALLED, BUT IT IS AWARENESS THAT BRINGS YOU TO THIS PLACE, THE KNOWING OF WHAT A GOOD FEELING IS SO THAT YOU CAN MATCH YOURSELF TO THAT, YOU CAN REACH FOR THAT. YES, IT IS A GIFT OF YOURS.

Liz: That's nice to hear because I can imagine for some people, and like I've experienced in my past, sometimes a good feeling isn't really a good feeling, it's a lower vibration, especially when it comes to substance abuse or whatnot. I think people might have to be clear on what a good feeling is.

Seth: Yes, there are many places, there are many steps to get to the place, there is the awareness around your emotion, of what a good feeling is, but there is also the knowing that you have a choice, in every moment you are making choices, that it is not outside of you. This is something of which you are deeply aware. And then allowing spirit to bring opportunities, experiences, excitement, future probabilities to you in your next best step. And so that if it makes you joyful to dream of a place where there is winter, this is your next best step.

Liz: And we can trust that it will unfold to what you were mentioning earlier about our soul's plan. If we're true with our resonance.

Seth: It is all about your vibration, about you living your life in expanded energy, about you living your life in your light paths, choosing out of your dark paths, consciously, deliberately, until it becomes a subconscious response. Simple, yes?

Liz: Yes, yes, yes... it is, its very simple and its different than 20 years ago and before, making plans and setting goals, doing everything you can to reach them, especially and there are a lot of people that still operate like that.

Seth: And it is not wrong. I do not wish to state that it is wrong, I get into trouble from Her when I state right and wrong, I do not wish to do that with Her today, but it is not the wrong, it is the energy on the planet, the male energy on the planet is all about planning and future outcomes, the female energy is about how do I make this moment better? And your planet has shifted and so this is what is supported now, this is the path to purpose, this is the path to love, joy, abundance, health, happiness. But, you are all safe and there are no wrong decisions, only growth opportunities, but you are still safe.

21:40 Liz: And what about past resonances, resonances from past experiences in your current now, when you have beliefs or thoughts that are in you, that are subconscious, you know, you do the same ... here's an example, I want to meet somebody, like a partner, a husband, someone to enjoy life with and I have wanted to meet them for like almost 10 years. So, I make my lists, I've made 40 lists, I've tweaked the lists, I've learned more about myself, so I'm growing, but its funny because I still get this feeling that I'm getting this same experience, over and over and over again. And so I look at myself and I think, there must be something in my belief system or in my resonance that is attracting this same situation over and over again and I am assuming a lot of people out there maybe experience that in love relationships or in work or family dynamics, the same thing over and over again, but we want to evolve and have a different experience, so I picked up tools along the way, like EFT / tapping to change the resonance, is there any validity to that or are some of us just meant to have, is that a part of my plan?

23:40 Seth: Well, all of it is valid, all of it valid for the time in which you learned it. Emotional Freedom Technique is a significant tool for changing, for moving energy blocks out of

THE BODY. BUT HERE IS WHERE YOU HAVE BROUGHT YOURSELF TO THIS MOMENT, WITH THIS NEW THOUGHT, THAT YOU MUST REACH FOR A BETTER FEELING AND YOU MUST TAKE THE NEXT BEST STEP. THIS IS THE WAY TO CHANGE YOUR VIBRATION. AS YOU SHIFT YOUR PERSONAL VIBRATION, YOU ATTRACT TO YOU THE VIBRATION OF A LOVER WHO IS A MATCH. AND SO, YOU BRING YOURSELF TO THIS PERFECT PLACE AND I HAVE SCANNED YOUR PICTURES AND THERE IS LOVE IN YOUR PLAN, BUT YOU MUST BRING YOURSELF TO THIS PLACE OF VIBRATIONAL MATCH. BUT YOU WILL NOT MANIPULATE, MUSCLE, WRING IT INTO SUBMISSION, YOU WILL PLACE FOCUS ON YOU, ON SELF. BUT THERE IS NO BELIEF SYSTEM THAT IS BLOCKING LOVE COMING TO YOU, THERE IS ONLY THE PERFECT, PERFECT WALKING OF YOUR PATH. YOU HAVE A TECHNIQUE NOW, YES?

25:54 Liz: Umm, a technique?

SETH: YES, FOR CREATING THE PERFECT OUTCOMES THAT YOUR SOUL YEARNS FOR.

Liz: Well, I guess, I'm learning to become more compassionate towards myself and other people, like the SolePath, that is the technique you're referring to?

SETH: IT IS WHAT YOU SAID TO ME IN THE BEGINNING, **I will reach for a better feeling thought and take my next best step, but you will also feel peaceful, you will feel peaceful it is only an experience**, THERE IS SO MUCH DRAMA ATTACHED TO NOT ACCOMPLISHING GOALS, I DID NOT FIND THE PERFECT MAN, I DIDN'T WIN THE LOTTERY, I'M NOT A MILLIONAIRE, I DON'T OWN AN ISLAND, I'M NOT DRIVING A FERRARI; ULTIMATELY, NONE OF THIS MATTERS AT ALL. IT IS HOW YOU FEEL AS YOU FLOW THROUGH LIFE, MOMENT BY MOMENT, AND

YOU ARE THERE NOW. IT IS WHY I HAVE ASKED YOU TO COME TO THIS
CONVERSATION WITH ME, YES. IT IS TIME, YES?

Liz: I'm very honoured, so thank you.

SETH: AND WE ARE COMPLETE.

If—

By Rudyard Kipling

If you can keep your head when all about you

Are losing theirs and blaming it on you,

If you can trust yourself when all men doubt you,

But make allowance for their doubting too;

If you can wait and not be tired by waiting,

Or being lied about, don't deal in lies,

Or being hated, don't give way to hating,

And yet don't look too good, nor talk too wise:

If you can dream—and not make dreams your master;

If you can think—and not make thoughts your aim;

If you can meet with Triumph and Disaster

And treat those two impostors just the same;

If you can bear to hear the truth you've spoken

Twisted by knaves to make a trap for fools,

Or watch the things you gave your life to, broken,

And stoop and build 'em up with worn-out tools:

If you can make one heap of all your winnings

And risk it on one turn of pitch-and-toss,

And lose, and start again at your beginnings

And never breathe a word about your loss;

If you can force your heart and nerve and sinew

To serve your turn long after they are gone,

And so hold on when there is nothing in you

Except the Will which says to them: 'Hold on!'

If you can talk with crowds and keep your virtue,

Or walk with Kings—nor lose the common touch,

If neither foes nor loving friends can hurt you,

If all men count with you, but none too much;

If you can fill the unforgiving minute

With sixty seconds' worth of distance run,

Yours is the Earth and everything that's in it,

And—which is more—you'll be a Man, my son!

Desiderata
by Max Ehrmann

Go placidly amid the noise and the haste,
and remember what peace there may be in silence.
As far as possible, without surrender,
be on good terms with all persons.

Speak your truth quietly and clearly, and listen to others,
even to the dull and the ignorant; they too have their story.

Avoid loud and aggressive persons; they are vexatious
to the spirit. If you compare yourself with others,
you may become vain or bitter, for always
there will be greater and lesser persons than yourself.

Enjoy your achievements as well as your plans.
Keep interested in your own career, however humble;
it is a real possession in the changing fortunes of time.

Exercise caution in your business affairs, for the world is full of
trickery.
But let this not blind you to what virtue there is;
many persons strive for high ideals,
and everywhere life is full of heroism.

Be yourself. Especially do not feign affection.
Neither be cynical about love, for in the face of all aridity and
disenchantment;
it is as perennial as the grass.

Take kindly the counsel of the years,
gracefully surrendering the things of youth.

Nurture strength of spirit to shield you in sudden misfortune.
But do not distress yourself with dark imaginings
Many fears are born of fatigue and loneliness.

Beyond a wholesome discipline, be gentle with yourself.
You are a child of the universe no less than the trees and the stars;
you have a right to be here.

And whether or not it is clear to you,
no doubt the universe is unfolding as it should.
Therefore, be at peace with God,
whatever you conceive Him to be.

And whatever your labours and aspirations
in the noisy confusion of life, keep peace in your soul.
With all its sham, drudgery, and broken dreams,
it is still a beautiful world. Be cheerful. Strive to be happy.

- More than our physical body
- connect wisdom
- Meta Physical   DNA
  Collapsed Energy - Expanded
                              Energy
* Evolution Angel Todd Michelle
  "You have to ask for help"
- Ask before Sleep what you
  need

_____

_____

_____

_____

_____

_____

_____

_____

_____

_____

_____

_____

_____

_____

_____

_____

_____

_____

_____

_____

_____

_____

_____

_____

_____

_____

_____

_____

_____

_____

_____

_____

_____

_____

_____

_____

_____

_____

_____

_____

_____

_____

_____

_____

_____

_____

_____

_____

_____

_____

_____

_____

_____

_____

_____

_____

_____

_____

_____

_____

_____

_____

_____

_____

_____

_____

_____

_____

_____

_____

_____

_____

_____

_____

_____

_____

_____

_____

ABOUT THE AUTHOR

Dr. Debra is a spiritual philosophy teacher with a doctorate in metaphysical science. She is an ordained minister and a member of the American metaphysical doctors association and the Canadian institute of metaphysical ministers.

Dr. Debra's SolePath is inspirational teacher and spiritual mystic. It is this SolePath that allows her to connect, create and communicate the SolePath original body of work. Her core values and core energy are spirituality and connection, inspiration and communication.

Dr. Debra Ford is the co-founder of the SolePath Institute, along with her husband John. The SolePath Institute joyfully encourages everyone to know and understand their SolePath and live a beautiful life, filled with purpose and meaning. The SolePath Institute supports you on the journey of your life, helping you to take the next best step.

Dr. Debra Ford Msc.D

SOLEPATH INSTITUTE CONTACT

Our purpose at the SolePath Institute is to ask how may we serve you, how can we help?

How may we encourage you on your path to a beautiful life filled with purpose?

Website: www.SolePath.org

Email: info@SolePath.org

Mailing address: the SolePath Institute,
                 716 Brookpark Drive SW,
                 Calgary, Alberta, Canada,
                 T2W 2X4

Helpline: 403.998.0191
                 1.877.866.2086

Seeing, Getting

Made in the USA
Charleston, SC
21 April 2014